# GIVE US THIS DAY

# Marj Leegard

# GIVE US THIS DAY

*Joy!*

*Marj Leegard*

## Augsburg Fortress

Minneapolis

*To my daughters,*
*grand, great, and appended:*
*Laurie, Julie, Megan, Ashley, Kaitlyn, and Annie*

Cover design by Mike Mihelich.
Text design by James Satter.

ISBN 0-8066-3866-4

The paper used in this publication meets the minimum requirements of American National Standard for Information Sciences—Permanence of Paper for Printed Library Materials, ANSI Z329.48-1984.

Manufactured in the U.S.A.                                    AF 10-38664

03    02    01    00    99    1    2    3    4    5    6    7    8    9    10

# Contents

# Foreword

"How blessed we are to have friends whose recipes and faithful lives fill our notebooks," Marj Leegard writes in her column "It's in the book." Indeed. In the more than 50 "Give Us This Day" columns that have appeared in *Lutheran Woman Today* since March 1994, hundreds of thousands of us have been blessed by the words and wisdom of Marj Leegard.

"Doubt can come, but faith gives strength that defeats despair," Marj writes in "By faith." We trust Marj because she generously shares with us her humanity, her saint-and-sinnerness, her ordinary, extraordinary life.

Born in 1920, Marj married Jerome Leegard in 1942. A farm outside Detroit Lakes, Minnesota. has been their home since 1945. Their son, Jim, and his wife, Sharon, have two children and two grandchildren. Their daughter, Laurie, died when she was 27 years old, when Laurie and Joe's daughter, Megan, was 3 years old.

After Laurie's wedding, Marj found a note that Laurie left for Marj and Jerome. "Thank you for 20 beautiful years. I love you," it read. Marj writes, "We would have been as good parents as we could be without Laurie's gratitude, just as God is good to us without our thanks. . . . If our hearts help us remember the joy of that benediction for us, we will give it more often to God and our families."

Thanks, Marj. Thanks be to God.

—Sue Edison-Swift, Managing Editor
*Lutheran Woman Today*

# Cherishing everyday saints

# Nellie's cookies

Nellie made white sugar cookies. Not dinky little
dry circles but big, tender cookies sparkling with
sugar and lightly browned at the edges. When her
cookies were admired she said, "These are just
sour-cream rolled cookies. Nothing special."

But they were special. We who were young
and full of new ideas from the latest magazines,
planned desserts for church events. We'd plan
great monstrosities of cream cheese and blue-
berries, marshmallows and crumb crusts. Nellie
would write the recipes down and then say,
"I think I will make a few cookies."

Generous soul that she was, she would bring
both the featured dessert and a big blue speckled
roaster filled with cookies. Corners of white linen
napkins poked out as a border under the roaster
cover. We watched from behind the counter as our
husbands chose their lunches. With schoolboy
smiles they reached for Nellie's cookies, then saw
our disappointment and took a dessert, carefully
balancing a cookie on top.

Nellie made every cup of coffee we ever drank
in that church. It was not a matter of putting the
plug in the automatic coffee maker. She filled the
huge graniteware pots from the cans of water
brought from home. She lifted them to the stove,
and while she waited for the water to boil she
mixed her secret formula of egg, coffee, and cold
water, then carefully stirred this into the pot
of boiling water. The critical move never mastered

by amateurs was the progression from hot to boiling to not boiling over. After a few minutes of settling the grounds, the coffee was strained into another pot and pronounced ready to serve. This amber and gold brew, shining with faint dots of luminescence, has not been seen since the demise of egg coffee from those old coffee pots.

Nellie's sister, Christine, was the "talented and gifted one," it was said. She was the church organist for more than 50 years. When her 50th year arrived, we had a celebration. There were photographers from 250 miles away. The church was filled with guests who came back to the old home church to help mark this anniversary. There were flowers and cards, speeches, music, and a sermon that reminded us how good it is to serve in the church. Christine had never received a salary, only little "puddles of money" left on the corner of the organ at Christmas and Pentecost. When we retired the old pump organ, Christine retired, too. We put a bronze marker on the new organ to honor her.

When we thought about Christine, we remembered her in her black suit and pink satin blouse, with her black hat perched exactly straight on her white hair. Nellie, we remembered in her starched apron and her welcoming smile that said, "Come to the banquet."

When Nellie was very old and not quite coherent, she mourned her lack of sainthood—her "useless life." She had kept the big house clean and neat for her brothers and her parents and for Christine. She had spent hours every week with the mop and the dust cloth keeping the church immaculate between "Aid" cleanings and the janitor's quick tidying.

We did not put a brass marker on her coffee pot or claim her blue roaster as a church artifact. Perhaps we should have.

Somehow we failed to sense that Nellie, too, had a ministry. How could we have forgotten that when we visited a home filled with sickness or great joy or sorrow and Nellie's cookies were there? When our babies were small, Nellie never asked, "Girl or boy?" She knew. And she knew their names. "There is little Jimmy," she would say, "and he is such a good boy."

I asked Nellie once how she could remember all those names, and she looked at me with wonder. "How can you pray for them if you do not learn their names at Baptism?"

It is too late to thank Nellie in person or to speak to her about her special kind of ministry, since she is no longer around to hear. But there is still time to remind ourselves and others that recognition of all our faithful ministers is in itself a ministry. Today would be a good time to start.

# The tribute

There is a sheet of construction paper on my wall. The printing is not centered, but all huddled at the bottom, and way over to the right. At the top is the assignment: "An Outstanding Person." It says in second-grade pre-cursive writing:

- my grandma is a good rosemaler
- she teaches other people how to
- she tells good bibel stores
- she makes good lefse
- she makes good flat bread
- she is a good organ player

Julie Petrina Leegard, grade 2

Half the people in Becker County do *rosemaling*— a Norwegian folk-art style of painting. Most of them do it much better than I do. I am glad for that, as some of them were my students. Julie has a little trouble spelling "Bible," but no difficulty with "lefse." Anyone can make lefse. All it requires is a short-term memory regarding the mess it makes in the kitchen. Flat bread is lefse's second cousin once removed. My organ playing depends on mechanics, and the marvelous wizard who connects the chords, and the compassionate souls who produce music with only one note for the right hand. As Julie grows up, she will acquire better taste in music.

However, I do not have to be an expert to be an outstanding person in my granddaughter's life. I don't even have to be above average by the world's standards. I produce lefse with butter and sugar on it; music; stories; and on occasion a decorated, round-top trunk. For a brief period in a grandchild's life that beats astronauts, Barbie dolls, and baseball players. Grandchildren love and accept us in a way that no other person ever does.

But that is the way that God loves our giftedness. We can't all be evangelists. No matter how well we use our gifts for music, there always is someone who's better. Our small gifts seem just that. Too small for God to notice. But God, who gives us our gifts, watches over us as we use them, and blesses what we do.

On your page God has written, "An Outstanding Person." May your list be long as you use those gifts, for Jesus' sake.

# The sounds of the church

Can you see the sun just touching the Statue of Liberty as you look out from your tiny room? New York is a long way from the farm. And the Staten Island ferry is just beginning its journey. Up from the streets and across from the waves come the sounds of my country. Farm and city. My country. The church, the people of God, join the song.

Now the dawn leads into day along eastern ocean beaches. The places where the breakers roar and winds move the sand, people gain strength from the elemental movement of water and land. The artist gathers her brushes and begins to form a palette of grays and blues. Lights and darks. The writer sits before a blank page and shapes the opening line. The musician listens for the inner melody that will be music only if she makes a mark upon the staff. The people of God are creating. God has new voice.

Now the dawn moves inland to wake the stringed instruments, the banjo and the fiddle, and brings them back to tune. The jangling alarm clock adds to the rising sounds of the church. A couple moves in complicated rhythms to sterilize and attach and detach and record as milk moves on its way from cows and sweet-smelling alfalfa to 2 percent and whipping cream.

Children move down the driveway toward the bus in the early morning darkness. The bus lights flash a warning front and back: "Precious cargo. Stay back." The church enters the school system in the best way, within the hearts and minds of children. Carriers of the melody.

The dawn leads on across the mountains to the places where the sun warms all the year. It shines through the window on a sewing table where a baby quilt is finished. The prayer rises: "Oh, Lord, there are homeless babies." The people of God are answers to the prayer. The table already is piled with more pieces and more pins and more warm batting.

What is this sound? Where is the church? Who speaks? An editor might ask, "Have you seen the letters?" The treasurer would sigh, "Have you seen the projected shortfall?" The president would urge her board to think about changing ways to get the young to come, for she worries that part of the sound is missing.

And yet from across the continent and islands, the sound of the church is heard. Prayers and praise carried in the hands of mothers and fathers as they love their children into another day. Loud sounds of the glory of creation as hammers pound and computers click. Trucks roll out onto the freeway, and road machinery makes smooth the way. There are soft touches of washcloths and soap as refreshing baths are given in the nursing home. There is the reassuring pat between husband and wife who have greeted the morning together for so many years that they are almost surprised at another new day.

Everywhere. Everywhere the church, the people of God, follow the dawn into a new day. Do you have time for a cup of coffee while you listen?

# Tell the story

At our house, for years the Christmas season seemed to pass in a whirlwind of dishes into the dishwasher and dishes out, food into the oven and food onto the table, and leftovers cared for . . . all while lines of people waited at the bathroom door and wanderers with sleeping bags looked for empty spots.

The wonderful confusion was always nice, but still when our daughter called to ask if we could spend Christmas at their home, I was packing before I hung up the phone. "What is 700 miles," I asked myself, "if for once I didn't have to cook lutefisk and roll lefse?"

Our 3-year-old granddaughter had plans for our first evening—the night before Christmas Eve. She had been in her first Christmas program, and it was such a good experience that she wanted to repeat it. We were the audience chosen for the encore.

"Mama," Megan said, "you play piano, and Daddy, you take pictures." We practiced the proper motions to "Away in a Manger" until Megan pronounced us ready to begin.

"Poppa," she said, "you will be Jofusss and I will be Mary." I asked what part I should play, and she said, "You be the donkey," and we were off to Bethlehem-by-the-cedar-chest. Events moved swiftly for those upright, but for me on my aging knees the time from prophecy to fulfillment was long.

"Poppa, go way down to the end of the hall and be all the Wise Men. You sing so loud." I thought that with the arrival of the three kings, I might be elevated to carrying a gift, so I asked what I would do. Sedate and serene, Megan said, "You will be the camel."

Suddenly the pageant was over and Megan said, "You have been such good children, I will read you a story." She ran to the kitchen and came back with the Advent calendar.

All of the little windows on the calendar were open except the one for the next day, Christmas Eve. Megan told the story, window by window, until she came to the one for this day. "No room! Go to the barn!" she said sternly. Then she looked down into our faces and she could not bear it. "But the baby Jesus is born," she said. "I peeked."

We have all had glimpses of grace. We have peeked. Some have great knowledge of the story and others have simply peeked. But we all know that God entered our world. As we look into the faces of those around us, may we be moved to share the news.

# Pass the Thanksgiving

Are you an "over the river and through the woods" grandmother, with a 40-pound turkey roasting in the oven and three different kinds of freshly baked pie cooling on the pantry shelves? Few of us are. Because we are not that grandmother, Thanksgiving gatherings are not quite what we think they once were.

Memories. Wonderfully roasted, crackly-brown turkey skin. Crisp, tart pickles and mashed potatoes with puddles of butter in the center. People laughing and hugging, and aunts who insist on kissing all the kids—even the boys. Memories have a way of bundling together every good thing about many Thanksgivings, many holidays. So perhaps it's no surprise that when we live the reality of this celebration, with our microscopes trained on every detail, nothing seems as perfect as it was then.

When we are children the family is what it is: family. When we grow older we see the family as fragments, as memories. There are empty chairs. It is difficult to realize that there have always been empty chairs. The family that seemed so complete when we were kids was fragmented to our grandparents.

So, how can I celebrate the perfect family gathering? There are many ways! I return to the frame of mind I had when I was a child. This is the day.

These are the people. One friend, two relatives, or three neighbors. It doesn't matter.

Second, share stories. I can fill those empty chairs with wonderful memories. I can share the stories of Uncle Wilbur who gave babies sticks of gum (that were quickly removed by their more circumspect mothers) and who shared his ice cream with his dog.

Third, I accept what the day brings with joy. So I don't have a huge turkey—just think, I won't have to deal with scrubbing the roaster! If I have one kind of pie, I'll smile and say, "I believe I'll have apple."

Finally, I offer thanks for God's many blessings. If we can't be the grandmothers who live "over the river and through the woods," we can be the historians who say: "God was." "God did." "God always." "Jesus said." The past holds the present steady and makes the future possible. Pass the blessing along this Thanksgiving.

# By faith

"By faith, Martha . . ."

The centerpieces on the dining room tables at church are new and bright. Martha made them. The women of the Dorcas Circle prepared scraps and patched 100 lap robes. Martha was there cutting and stitching. Is there one who needs encouragement or company for a lonely task? Martha will be there.

Martha's red hair, shining blue eyes, and big smile are so beautiful that it is difficult to remember she and Clarence have been married for 53 years. That's Clarence over there, playing old tunes on his accordion while Martha goes from wheelchair to davenport with hugs, gathering requests and taking those who are able in the careful whirl of a long-remembered waltz. The smiles of her partners hold memories of places long tumbled away, friends from childhood, and feet once lithe and quick.

What force is it that has taken Martha and Clarence out for years on hot summer and icy winter days to play for people in a nursing home? What makes them help beyond help, and then help again?

I know the secret. I learned it long ago. It was a time of tragedy for them: a cruel accident that claimed one so young it was shattering and unbearable to friends, but what to parents? We had gathered to confirm on Sunday then to bury days later. Our heads were filled with fearful questions, and our hearts with deep doubt.

Sunday came again. There were Martha and Clarence, back among us by faith, even in the midst of their loss. Their faith answered our tortured question, "How can you bear it?" Laying aside every weight, by faith we go on.

Doubt can come, but faith gives strength that defeats despair. To live by faith is to become one of Hebrews' great cloud of witnesses who give strength to others. Martha gives strength to us. Whose faith gives witness to you?

# It's in the book

Do you have a favorite recipe book? Mine is a little handwritten notebook. On the inside cover it says, "From Peggy. Most of these I got from you in the first place." She made it for me when my own recipe books were destroyed in a fire. The recipes have names on them. "Mom's Meat Balls," "Donna's Coconut Treasure Cake," "Doris' Bars," "Marj's Chocolate Fudge" (which in my old book had been "Emma's Fudge"). I have added "Myrt's Salad Dressing" and pages of instructions for other projects—like 100 popcorn balls. Who can imagine making 100 popcorn balls anymore?

We all have ways of preserving recipes, some more orderly than others. We keep them—and keep adding to them—because they help us in our daily rounds of family care. By identifying the recipe with the person who introduced it to us, we remember the taste and smell and look of the finished product. When I want to make meatballs, I don't want some exotic, pineapple-scented, soy-sauced, garlic-flavored nuggets. I want "Mom's Meat Balls." Tested, tried, and true.

I have another book. It has no visible dimensions. I carry it in my head. If my little recipe notebook is stained and worn, this book I carry in my head is tattered to the 7th power. Its truths came into being in conflict, stress, sorrow, and fear. Its truths are tested and bear the names of the people from whom they were learned. It contains faith-in-daily-life wisdom, as interpreted by friends. And they take me through my daily rounds.

I learned from Jerry's quiet listening "being in full accord and of one mind" (Philippians 2:2b). There are faster ways to plan together but not better ways. Mary taught me to grieve when I didn't want to learn. She dealt with me "with patience, bearing with one another in love" (Ephesians 4:2b). John's page is filled with great joy, and his joy comes from the joy in Luke 24:52-53: "And they worshiped him, and returned to Jerusalem with great joy; and they were continually in the temple blessing God." John continually teaches me to see the joy.

My little book of recipes and my invisible book of directions for life are gifts from the experiences of others. How blessed we are to have friends whose recipes and faithful lives fill our notebooks.

# A wonderful gift

Miss Beck gave me a wonderful gift. I don't know
the exact moment she gave it to me. I don't remember its shape or content. I only know that the gift
was given sometime in our relationship as teacher
and pupil in the first grade.

We sat on little varnished chairs and listened
as she read, "By the shores of Gitchee Gumee, By
the shining Big-Sea-Water, Stood the wigwam of
Nokomis. Daughter of the Moon, Nokomis."

We repeated Longfellow's lines after Miss Beck.
Then, when we were back at our desks carefully
sticking pinholes into rough off-white construction
paper, the rhythm of the poem flowed through our
fingers and through the pin. At first, the shape
drawn on the paper was meaningless to us. We
made neat little holes on the drawn lines. Gradu-
ally we learned that we had completed the letter A.
Before we could go on to B we went back to the
poem and the dark forest and the "firs with cones
upon them."

Somewhere in the days of poetry and stories,
of tracing and sounding out, I learned to read.
Miss Beck gave me that wonderful lifelong gift.

For me, *teacher* is a title filled with meaning,
alive with many faces, carrying specific names in
memory. Ruth, who taught the littlest ones for 40
years and loved every day of it. Mrs. Simonson, who
cleared up the mystery of reading for boys who had
been puzzled for the first six years of school. I'm
sure you, too, recall beloved teachers.

Is it any wonder that Mary, weeping at the opened grave, responds to her name when she is addressed by her beloved teacher? In her grief and loneliness she could not think in resurrection terms—Savior, Redeemer, King. She heard her named called by one she loved. One who opened new ways of thinking. "Repent for the kingdom of heaven is upon you." "There must be no limit to your goodness, as your heavenly Father's goodness knows no bounds." "And when you stand praying, if you have a grievance against anyone, forgive him." "Set your troubled hearts at rest. Trust in God always; trust also in me."

So many things to remember. Our faith is nourished and strengthened by the rhythms of the liturgy, in the sounding out of the Bible study, in the quiet outlines of prayer. We may not be able to name the day that the teachings became alive, but we will not forget the teacher.

# Growing in grace

# Kettle covers

The man arrived early for the farm auction. His old friends were moving to town. The boxes were ready on the flatbed wagons. There was no extra room in the new, smaller house. No shop. An efficiency kitchen.

He hardly looked into the boxes, for they were always the same. Good covers for kettles. Why only the covers? Then he remembered that the kettles went on to another use. Some held geraniums on the porch steps. Some held oyster shells in the chicken coop. Some were nests for the banty hens the kids raised. Some were repaired and became welcome water sources in the yard. It was only the kettle covers that stayed unchipped. Only the covers that had no further function.

The kettle covers were placed with the other things, for the auctioneer knew that no one would buy a box of *only* covers. So a rusty old pie tin, a souvenir ashtray, and an advertising set of measuring spoons shared the box with the enameled covers.

As the auctioneer's melodious chant echoed through the yard, the man could not help himself. He held his number up and became the owner of another box of what his wife would label "JUNK"— if she saw it. Of course, she was right. He never did find a treasure in a box, but there was something more than the box there. There was the awkward pause in the bidding and his desire to keep things going for his old friends who could no longer farm. Sometimes he could bid the pace up and up and quit in time so that someone else had to figure out how to explain why he "dragged that home."

His wife had laid down the law. He wasn't even to think about bringing home any more auction stuff. So, following her direction, he didn't think about it as he hid his boxes in the barn.

So when time came to sell his farm, his grand-children found his collection of auction-sale acquisitions in the hayloft—still neatly packed in the boxes they had been in all these years. Along with the boxes and the dishes were chairs. The line of chairs stood in crooked heights and cobwebbed colors. Not one chair looked sturdy enough for use even if the dust could be brushed away.

In a made-up story, these waiting chairs would be cherry and oak and 100 years old. And kettle covers would become the latest rage for collectors. But this haymow is not the scene for a fairy-tale ending. This haymow is part of the ordinary world.

And the ordinary world decrees that not all seems to fit into a neat scheme in life. Once we worked and produced and earned. Now the kettle is gone and the cover is left. We dip into our savings and wonder whether we'll have enough to last. We wake with a start. "We are late!" And then we lie back wondering, "Late for what?" No more school bus. No more milk truck. No more hurrying.

Our children are grown and capable of telling us what to do. We are now the grandmothers and great-grandmothers in the generation pictures. We are the covers. We can sit on the sidelines, like that row of chairs, and mourn for our former glory. We can let ourselves be covers unchipped, undented, and unused. Or we can be the kettles that are never assigned to the useless and unnecessary corner. It doesn't matter that we no longer bubble on the stove from morning until night. We've *done* that! We still make nesting places and produce blooms and provide water for the thirsty.

God has plans for each of us, for all of our days. We listen as we pray. We listen as we read. We listen as we hear the gospel. While we listen, we hear our names called. There is today for you a place where you are needed. Where you can be the feet, the hands, the heart, the generosity, the love of Christ in God's creation. "He gives power to the faint, and strengthens the powerless" (Isaiah 40:29). God's children are never discarded. Never useless. Never too old.

# Golden marriage

She sat down in the easy chair and let the festivities around her wind down. The gold tinsel on the evergreen trees bordering the yard glistened in the setting sun. Jimmie was packing up his music-making equipment. The laughing young women were finishing the cleanup in the kitchen.

Her granddaughters flopped down on the floor beside her chair. "It was a nice party," Megan said, "Except for the pickles. Pickles are supposed to be salty and sour and taste like garlic. Sweet. Aaaaagh."

"The music was worse than the pickles," Julie said. "The music you *had* to listen to. The pickles you could leave on your plate. I asked Jimmie to play some good music, and he said he was playing what you and Grandpa liked."

As the girls left for other pursuits, she saw her husband standing on the sidewalk, telling the last of the guests he was glad they came. He stood as straight and tall as he had the first day she met him.

Her mind went back to their wedding day, and she wondered how anyone could make promises that lasted such a long time: "So long as ye both shall live." She supposed that they had said "plight thee my troth," which was easier then because in that lightheaded moment before the altar she hadn't the faintest idea what "plighting her troth" meant.

At the celebration today nobody had asked her the secret of a long marriage, but she thought about what she would have said.

How could she have known that he would hurry through his work to come in and rock babies when they were sick? Would she have held valuable his penchant for getting up earlier and working harder and keeping at it longer? That didn't seem as important as his blue eyes when she was making those impossible promises.

Family. She thought they had a new beginning, as new and shiny as the kettles they unpacked. But in their marriage they had unpacked so many things. His ethnic heritage and her food dislikes. His saving ways and her urge to travel. They made chicken pie the way his grandmother made it— crust on both the top and bottom. Her Yankee ancestors groaned at the thought.

She felt rested and got up to thank her daughter-in-law and friends in the kitchen. She was glad no one had asked her the secret of a long and happy marriage. She didn't know any secrets, only the truth. All God's children are cared for in every way. And sometimes there are golden wedding anniversaries.

# Christmas comes in quiet

There is no one in the world who was told more often than I to "keep quiet" as a child. My mother said it. My teachers said it. "Hush!"

Psalm 46:10 has words for me: "'Be still . . . !'" The Contemporary English Version has this great translation: "Our God says, 'Calm down, and learn that I am God!'" Silence is hard to learn, but quiet is necessary.

I wonder about the angels readying themselves for their Christmas concert, the very first Christmas concert. There was no pre-concert hush in Bethlehem. People gathered for a family reunion of sorts, though one often does not attend a family reunion to be taxed. There probably was a babble of people recalling their journeys, sharing news and tax complaints—no quiet for a concert.

It is quiet in the stable. The angels look at the sleeping baby, the young, tired mother, and watchful Joseph. The angels decided against opening the heavens here.

Away from Bethlehem the hillside pasture lies calm and quiet in the evening stillness. The sheep are resting. No ewes call for their lambs—all are safely near. The shepherds watch beside the dim and dying fire so that no harm comes to the flock. Herders on this hill are ready for the voice of God, and God's voice comes.

The shepherds' ears, nurtured by the soft bleating of sheep and the occasional conversation of other shepherds, are keen for the first sounds of the host on high. The sounds come.

As Christmas comes to me and you, is it strange that it comes in quiet? In dim light? In loneliness? As we watch over those in our care?

God comes! Today there is born a Savior! No more "hush, be quiet." Now is the time for praise and glory, light and celebration. "The shepherds returned, glorifying and praising God for all they had heard and seen" (Luke 2:20). We can do no less.

# A century of life

Ashley is the new baby and grandbaby and great-granddaughter and great-great-grandchild in our family. She has big dark eyes. A startling amount of black hair frames her face. Her great-great-grandmother Edna was born almost at the turn of the 19th century, and little Ashley, God willing, will count time in the 21st century.

Babies fill us with wonder. They smile and make gentle sounds, and we are ecstatic. There is no fragrance on earth so lovely as the smell of a clean baby nestled on our shoulders. The centuries have been made alive with these miracles of God's creation.

We trace Ashley's lineage from her father in little lines on the family tree, while other grandparents and great-grandparents trace her line in other directions. All the while, her genes are pushing out the dark hair to make her the blonde that she will become.

In all the years of time that families have loved children into being and then nurtured them to adulthood, in all those years there have been moments of great joy and moments of anguish and tears. The powerful force of life, that life-breath of God, moves with us down the eons of time.

Ashley was content to sit in our laps in the first months of her life, but now she wants her mother. It is no use to remind her that this kindly man is the great-grandfather who will buy her bubble gum and a green tractor and take her riding in the pony cart. She puckers up her little face and tries to remember the sound that gets action. Ah, yes. Cry. And cry she does. We wish that she would never have to cry again, but we know that she will.

In all this force of life and love there is fear. Fear that takes for its lament Rachel weeping for her children. We cry out with the depredations of the psalmist against his enemies. We shout into the wind and howl into the ocean waves. This life is precious. All life is God-given. No more bullets. No more starvation. No more cruelty of speech and hand. No more alien substances leeching life away. No more unchecked disease. No more poisoned air and water. We search for a platform for our voices. We dig for words with strength and meaning.

God has spoken from the mountain: "Thou shalt not kill."

# Boots and pitchers and things

I don't suppose I thought of it as coveting. Maybe
*wanting* and all the words that followed: *hoping
for, begging for, wishing for.* Yes, and *praying for.*
I wanted boots. Brown leather boots, with a pocket
on the side and a knife in the pocket. A tiny folded
jackknife. Boots with metal hooks for fast lacing.
And I was a girl! That was part of the problem.
I didn't want to *be* a boy, but boots would assuage
the inequity a little.

There was also the problem of what to wear
with the boots if I had them. Does one wear boots
with a dress? Girls wore dresses in 1930 (when I
was doing my wishing). One movie star wore pants
and looked great—great and absolutely scandalous.

But, of course, one wore breeches with boots.
Those lovely pants that flared out at the sides and
fitted tightly into the boot tops. I wanted breeches,
too, but I had more sense than to mention that. The
boots were not immediately forthcoming as it was.

It is difficult to know why I want what I want.
I know the longing is there. Somehow I think I am
going to be a better person when I have that elusive
wished-for thing. *Ha!*—three-way mirrors in a
dressing room ought to dispel my notions of great
improvement!

Shelves of old pottery pitchers have not made our house a stopping place on the Library Club's tour of homes, and fancy kettles did not make me a gourmet cook. But the anticipation and realization of pitchers and kettles and boots (without a knife pocket!) were joyous experiences.

God commands that I do you no harm by my wanting and wishing *and* that I do myself no harm by forgetting where my treasure is: ". . . store up for yourselves treasures in heaven, where neither moth nor rust consumes and where thieves do not break in and steal. For where your treasure is, there your head will be also" (Matthew 6:20-21).

May I remember that when you and I both reach for the same squatty brown pitcher at the next flea market.

# *Insights in faith*

# Benediction

The day before the wedding I was doing some last-minute cleaning in the entryway when our daughter, Laurie, came out and sat down on the step. She motioned for me to sit beside her. As I shut off the vacuum cleaner I muttered to myself, "Surely she is not going to change her mind when I have baked a zillion tiny cookies. Or can it be that she wants to know something more about sex? And I have little knowledge and even less willingness to discuss it further." I sat down beside her.

"Mom," she said, "I don't want to tell you good-bye tomorrow night. I don't want to leave for my new home crying, and I don't want to tell Daddy that I don't want to tell him good-bye. Will you promise not to come after us as we leave? Just let us slip away." I promised, and we did our crying ahead of time. We were happy We loved our daughter's choice. But we were sad because the time had gone too swiftly from little girl to grown-up. I went back to my preparations.

The wedding day was cold. Thirty degrees below zero—actual temperature, not windchill. The wedding was just as she and Joe had planned, a Christmas wedding with bridesmaids in red velvet, decorated Christmas trees, and a Norwegian buffet.

As the bride and groom were walking toward the door, my husband, Jerome, said, "Let's go home." We knew Laurie and Joe planned to change clothes at our house, so we could catch them there. My desire for one more hug overcame my promises,

39

and I followed my husband to the cloak room. People stopped us. "Such a nice couple. It was a beautiful wedding." "My, we watched them grow up together." "Storybook romance. They never did go with anyone else, did they?" We said, "Yes, yes, yes, and no," and finally began putting on scarfs and caps and coats and overshoes and mittens, but then got stopped in our bundled-up condition.

People wanted to discuss how lovely the wedding cake was and ask if we had the recipe for those almond rusk things?

We finally made it out to the car and the starter ground away with no enthusiasm and very little spark. On about the 15th grind, the car started and we drove home. There was no car in the yard. There were two girls helping with the cleaning up. Jerome asked, "Have they been here?" and the girls said, "Yes." Jerome said, "Did they say anything?" "No."

Then the plaintive question, "Did they say goodbye?" The girls smiled and nodded. Jerome persisted "Did they say to tell us anything?" and the girls said, "No."

We were soon alone. More alone than we had been in the 36 years of having a child or two in the house. Laurie's wedding dress was on her bed. Joe's tux was hanging on the bathroom door. Jerome went to bed and when I came in he was way over on the far side. Usually he took his two-thirds right in the middle and threw spread and blankets in all directions. The spread had not been touched. He was a lonely father of the bride with his face turned toward the wall. I turned the spread back on my side and there was a piece of paper. I turned the light on and read it aloud. "Dear Mom and Dad," it said. "Thank you for 20 beautiful years. I love you. Laurie."

Jerome sat up and said, "Do we have anything in the house to eat besides wedding cookies? I am hungry."

We would have been as good parents as we could be without Laurie's gratitude, just as God is good to us without our thanks. But what a wonderful benediction thankfulness is at the close of the day or of a part of life. *Thank you for the beautiful years.* If our hearts help us remember the joy of that benediction for us we will give it more often to God and our families.

# New math

Misty was our little Welsh pony. She raised our daughter and got our grandchildren off to a good start. Misty's disposition was not sunny. She was opinionated and independent, but it is good for children to learn that their whims and orders are not automatically obeyed.

Misty lived a good life, growing so broad across her back that youngsters' little feet often stuck straight out when they rode. Misty liked both tuna-fish and peanut-butter sandwiches. She distrusted oats—evidently we interrupted her idyll relaxation in the summer sun too often with a bucket of oats. Misty had a mind of her own. She would trot gracefully off with her young charges, but when the rider changed direction to indicate a ride might be over she would, at the sight of the barn door, put on her race-horse exhibition—thrilling for old hands but terrifying for novices.

When Misty was very old she died and was buried in the shade of the crab apple tree. That should be the end of Misty's story, but one 6-year-old granddaughter wanted a stone on Misty's grave. "A stone must be there," Megan insisted, "else where will we plant flowers?" Grandfather mixed some quick and easy cement, shaped a form, and gathered his little helpers to make a flat marker. They spooned and filled and smoothed and made ready for the inscribing. With a twig Megan printed "MISTY" and the year of Misty's birth, 1963.

"Now I'll put the plus and 1989," she said. "You don't need a plus," I said, brushing away the mosquitoes.

Megan paused, twig in hand. "I want 1963 plus 1989," she said.

"Hold on a minute!" I said, "Just put one date on one side and the other in the other corner."

"It has to have a plus," she insisted.

"This is not arithmetic," I countered.

Megan turned to me and said quietly, "All the stones in the cemetery at church have a plus." And in the air she drew a cross.

Of course we must have a plus. That is the most important part.

# This day and this place—joy?

We were rattling along the interstate heading west, just the four of us—if you count the cat as one of us. He was riding in regal haughtiness like a king reviewing his troops as he watched approaching traffic through the little window above the driver's seat in our motor home.

Our granddaughter, having just turned 14, was excited about spending "family week" at Bible camp with us. Suddenly she was fearful. "I won't know anyone," she wailed. We were 400 miles closer to Custer, South Dakota, than to home. Grandfather kept driving, and the cat carefully watched his army pass in review. I tried to explain that kids from all over the country were coming to camp and that they would each need a friend. Finally, as that fear subsided, Megan had one last ultimatum. "I will not ride horseback," she said.

Ten minutes after we were welcomed into the camp, she had three friends. The very next morning she came into the room where I was with the adults and whispered, "I need you to sign this so I can ride horseback."

A few days later I was searching through my bag and discovered a little note. It said, "Dear Gram, Thank you for bringing me to this place." My mind went back to the time when her mother was small. She had just had an injection and it hurt. Her eyes were filled with tears, but she looked up as the nurse pressed the bandage in place and said,

"Thank you."

We do not have that grace very often. We find ourselves in places we would not have chosen, at a time of life that seems not as good as earlier times, in a position not quite the one we dreamed of having. Our first thought is seldom to thank. Our list of complaints is ready—and long. We want to be younger. We want to be stronger. We want to be the best and the brightest and the most talented. We want to be somebody else, someplace else. It is hard to see the joy in this place, in this day, while we enjoy our misery.

Two little girls, through tears and fears, help me to remember to say, "Thank you." There is joy! "I wish you joy in the Lord always. Again I say: all joy be yours" (Philippians 4:4, Revised English Bible).

# Freedom

The girls were 10 and 11 and tired of setting up house-keeping in the basement. Something not too far away from Gram but just far enough would be ideal. A tree house, ranch-style, two bedrooms, and a living room would be nice. Megan chose a tree that grew three tree trunks from a single root. Julie began to carry lumber and tools.

They discovered that three tree trunks made a triangle and the plans changed. When the floor was finished, it was too low, too small, and too hard to remove. "Let's just move up higher," they said, "and leave the bottom as a basement." In scrounging for material they found some netting fence. Great! They'd raise chickens downstairs and live upstairs.

Their toil on warm summer days soon came to fruition. With an old sheet for walls, they were cozy, protected from wind and bugs, and free to read in the quiet of their own, now one-room, abode. The chickens were still in the future.

Freedom to be alone, away from duty and super-vision, feels wonderful to most of us. The freedom of our own space gives stability to the difficult every-day world. We need a tree house open to sky and closed to bugs. We need dreams yet unrealized.

In Galatians 5:1, Paul says, "It is for freedom that Christ has set us free" (Revised English Bible). We are not free from *have to* so that we can curl up and *don't do*. We have the Christ-given freedom to *want to*.

That freedom sends us searching for tools, exercising talents that we hardly knew we had, changing directions to meet needs, and beginning the day excited about our dreams.

The girls are growing up. Would you believe that the tree house is growing also? As the tree stretches upward, the house moves along. There are still no chickens in the basement, but there is that place that represents freedom.

Granddaughters will go on to new freedoms, new dreams. Grandpa and Grandma will leave the house undisturbed. It is good to have a marker to remind us that "it is for freedom that Christ has set us free."

# Groundedness

It's that time of year again: The time that tradition tells us—and a national holiday reminds us—to visit the cemeteries. It is not that we follow tradition to the familiar grave sites, but that tradition and holiday have followed us for generations while we decorate and remember.

In those months when there are no snowbanks, there are some who can walk out after worship to pick off a dead geranium blossom, pinch back the petunias, and pull out the stray weed at the headstone that reads, "Daughter" or "Husband" or "Baby." It is a family visit to a family that was, a family group that lives in memory. A family forever changed, not only by death but by the lives those remembered ones brought to us.

Children play among the stones and try to read the faint marks on the oldest thin, white, limestone tablets. Older children show young cousins the stone that has a tiny photograph covered with glass embedded in the granite. Life gains an added dimension: There is not only now and tomorrow but also yesterday.

When we are planting vines and flowers, I mumble, "Why are we doing this? She is not here. She is not here." And then I know that God created her body and gave us the gift of a daughter for earth years and for eternity. There is thankfulness in the rush of color, the blooms of the flowering crab-apple trees. We must have a place of remembrance, and in the old cemetery we find one place.

Florists remind us many times during the year that flowers speak of love. Our plant with the perfect pink hearts in the shade of the headstone speaks of love. When the little children help and ask questions, when the teenagers lend strong backs and arms to lugging plants and water pails, when grandparents tell stories as they work, there is groundedness. Death is not some violent theatrical event on television, but a part of life. We can expect death and we can expect the shepherd's rod and staff to comfort us (Psalm 23).

Memorial Day is on the calendar because the heart longs to remember. After a season of winter, it is time.

# Forever and ever again

Our friend John's little grandson wrote a declaration in olive-green marking pen. When the green ran out, he finished in red. I don't know what the occasion was that moved him to share his faith, but share it he did.

> I love Jesus better then ice cream even tho I don't obay him and do the things I should and he loves me so much. And he's my father for ever and ever again and I will be his kid.

There are poets, liturgists, theologians, and lyricists who might put confession and praise in different words, but this simple expression says it well. John's grandson has the Trinity figured out. It will not be difficult for him to read John 14:9, "Jesus said to him, 'Have I been with you all this time, Philip, and you still do not know me? Whoever has seen me has seen the Father.'"

We are told to become like little children, but when did you last think of yourself as God's kid?

"Forever and ever again" is a long time for a little boy. It is a long time for us, also. We end our Lord's prayer "forever and ever." He ends his bold statement with "forever and ever again." That must be a very long time!

"Forever and ever again" takes account of the sometimes frightening thought that time and space are more complicated than we imagined. And yet in all our knowledge there still is the overriding truth:

We love Jesus even though we don't obey him. Oh, little kid, you are not alone in that. We join you daily in our own prayers and weekly in the gathered confession that opens the worship of our congregations. How can we love Jesus and disobey him?

What shall we do? The world is big, and space is expanding. And our capacity for sin grows ever more devious. We lose sight of the simple and uncomplicated. Wisdom can be lost in the stuff of age.

Thank you, little member of the Graf family, for reminding us that we will always, "forever and ever again," be God's kid.

# Alice by the water fountain

Alice and I were the only ninth graders taking both biology and chemistry. It was not because we were such good students that we wanted to be challenged. It was because we didn't like home ec.

Baked apples filled with cooked oatmeal and touted as a breakfast dish made us sick, and our teacher returned our buttonhole samples with the question, "What is this?" Besides, we had both decided that there must be better things to do in life than housework. In 1935 that was not a common idea.

We went into Miss Daley's exotic classroom with its smells and charts and prepared for two hours of mystery. She chose to begin with butter-flies, and I sat back happily ready, for butterflies I understood. And then the world came crashing down around my ears.

I peeked across the row to see how others were reacting, but there was only calm. Miss Daley began to explain orders and families and *lepidoptera,* I think. And I thought butterflies just grew from caterpillars! That was mystery enough for me. But here was total chaos. Butterflies were not created butterflies but hatched out of some complex plan of definite order which it seemed I was expected to memorize.

Then it was time for chemistry.

Alice and I grew up before the advent of required science classes. Before field trips. Before children's programming on TV explained the workings of the world. Here we were, fresh from total disillusion about butterflies, and about to learn that water is not water but molecules of hydrogen and oxygen. I never thought I would long to be back in home ec., ripping out crooked bias tape.

The two hours came to an end, and I stumbled out into the hall and stopped by the water fountain to wait for Alice. I was a skinny ninth grader torn from my moorings. Alice came with her blond braids swinging and a big smile.

"Alice," I asked, "did you know anything about this?"

"No," she said, "But isn't God wonderful?"

# A Christmas for all creation

The time was set for supper. When lutefisk is ready, it is *ready*. They were doing what newlyweds do: heading home for Christmas Eve. And he was late coming in from the barn.

She waited the full extent of her patience and then bundled up to find out the cause of the delay. It was cold and dark. The snow squeaked under her boots, but the barn was warm and dimly lighted from the yellow glow of a kerosene lantern. She slipped inside. He was not hurrying at all.

Belle and Tootsie and Lovely were pulling choice bits from the enormous piles of hay in their mangers and tossing them high in the air before they began their thoughtful cow-chew. Why, when time was so short, was he feeding again *after* milking?

The big team had oats in the feed boxes. They were stamping their feet and blowing into the grain with exuberant great snorts. He was holding a pail of skim milk for his favorite horse and talking to her.

His bride opened her mouth to shout out her impatient questions when she heard him saying, "Merry Christmas, Ruthie. Merry Christmas, Ruby and Bob and Tony." Each horse looked up to receive the Christmas message he gave.

She quietly shut the door and went back to the house to wait as long as it took.

She was a town kid. Animals were fearsome and a nuisance. He was a farmer and respecter of creation. "And God made . . . the cattle according to their kinds. And God saw that it was good" (Genesis 1:25, Revised Standard Version). This farmer saw animals not only as good, but as creatures meant to share in the wonderful news that Christ came to earth in a manger bed, in a barn shared with donkeys and sheep and doves.

We share our world with squirrels and cats. With horses and dogs. With cows and sheep and pigs. With animals in the zoo and animals living out of our sight. With deer and moose and tiny chickadees. With orioles and cardinals and blue jays. With chipmunks and goldfish and all created kinds. How shall we greet them on Christmas?

# My child, too

LeAnn was born not with the newborn ecstasy of life, but with the inevitability of death casting a shadow around her beautiful head. Everyone knew her life would be short, and it hurt to feel the pain of her parents and little brothers. We shared tears with the grandparents and aunties. We wanted to know "WHY?" and we asked the baby's parents what our pastor said when he visited.

"He didn't *say* anything," Pam said. "He just put his arms around us, and we all cried." So often we want words to go before us to make the pathway smooth and fragrant and lovely. But God's promise is "presence" on every pathway we walk.

LeAnn's baptism came early on her journey. She came to church dressed in white. Her lovely little face was framed in the ruffles of her bonnet, and she was cozy in her handmade shawl. Pastor Kropp held her in his arms and said to us all, "She is our baby to care for and to love."

We have heard that said in many ways. The service for Holy Baptism in *Lutheran Book of Worship* bids the congregation to say, "We welcome you into the Lord's family. We receive you as fellow members of the body of Christ, children of the same heavenly Father, and workers with us in the kingdom of God."

That thought, in formal and informal expression, took on a new meaning as LeAnn's care became more difficult. Her brothers with fists full of flowers for her, and her mother and father talking to her as they soothed and caressed—all helped make it possible for professional caregivers to know her as a beloved baby and not as a difficult duty.

But it was Pam's exchange with a fellow parishioner who thought he would be more comfortable if he did not see LeAnn that gave the words added meaning for me. Pam simply said, "She is your baby, too."

Those words follow me around my congregation and community. Because children have needs, they are my needs, too. I cannot give up on the "rascals," for they are my rascals, too. The words follow me into the world. Those hungry babies are my babies, too.

Thank you, LeAnn. After just 18 months, your life on earth ended. Your blessing lives on even as you have eternal life, the promise of baptism.

# A painter's prayer

Heavenly Father, let me paint a picture that will define a word. A picture so clear and true that ever after it will be said, "Church? The picture says it all."

I will put blue on my palette for the sky. White and gray for the tall church on the hilltop. Darkest green for the fir trees that stretch past the steeple's height. There will be yellow for the sun shining on the gravestones that stand so closely by.

Or shall I place my easel inside the church that leaves a pane of glass without the stained-glass artist's touch so that the mountains can be seen? Or should I go to the hot veld in Africa and sketch the low stone walls with roofs that barely bear the name?

Or might I choose the chapel surrounded by science and history and music and students? And, too, there is the room in an office building where worship shapes the day and the deliberations.

I have gray on my palette. I could put on canvas the inside of the church with walls of cement slabs, rough edges of cement extruding from the places where workmen filled the forms. Then I remember the little Camp Fire girl, whose church this wasn't, saying, "But this isn't pretty!" And the answer from our tour-guide priest, "Ah, but you should see it when the people come with all their colors and their smiles. Then it is beautiful." Oh Lord, you know I can't paint people. They won't stay still while I shut one eye and measure with my thumb and finger as if I know what I am doing. People move from the inside of the church to houses and apartments and hospitals and benches in deserted parks. They go to work and school and gatherings of others like themselves. They are only here long enough to be sent there by your call. And if I take my brushes to follow them, they point to people's needs, and wonder at my idleness.

No matter how many colors and shapes and shadows and canvasses I use, I cannot paint church. God, church is yours to define.

Include me in your definition, for Jesus' sake. Amen.

# Bible breakfast

Candlelight dinners are nice. Picnics in the park make wonderful memories. But breakfast is the best meal of the day. Many restaurants serve breakfast all day and all night. There are people who breakfast once a week with friends, and groups that hold meetings over that savory meal.

Breakfast can be a guilty look in the general direction of the kitchen before scrambling out the door. It can be a quick something out of the toaster, eaten on the run. It can be a glass of juice and a cup of coffee—and a promise to find something nutritious later. It can be a bowl of grain glorified in shape and color, with nuts, raisins, brown sugar, and honey.

Some of the best breakfasts are fed by our memory, like the farm breakfast consumed on a winter morning four hours after the start of the day. There were thick slices of homemade bread-turned-toast and crisp, home-cured bacon. Fresh eggs sprinkled with pepper. Tart and purple chokecherry jelly. Soft molasses cookies with shiney frosting. The memory almost makes up for today's store-bought, limp toast served with an occasional egg.

A very long time ago, on retreat, Mrs. Moldrem told us, "Bible study and devotions are like breakfast." That thought stuck. Our bodies need breakfast, and our souls need Bible study and devotions.

We can have good intentions about prayer and reading our Bibles. Time gets away and we rush out the door with only a guilty glance toward the place that might have anchored our day.

We can find time for that "Bible breakfast" at moments other than the morning, and still enjoy the feast. We can join a friend or group of friends for the prayer and reading that breaks the fast. We can embellish our study and our devotions with varying translations and study aids that sweeten and deepen our understanding.

We may find ourselves nostalgic about the family gathered around the fireplace, with long-ago children and parents of our dreams, but that will never fill our souls with the life-saving word. Memories are wonderful and can encourage, guide, and comfort. But memories alone cannot feed our souls. However we gather, however we read, however we are changed, we breakfast in the very best way with our Bibles every day.

# Abundant, flowing water

No one appreciates water flowing from a faucet as much as someone who remembers water pails. Those white, enameled pails were permanently orange on the inside from the iron in the water. Tin dippers gave the water a flavor that cannot be duplicated. For deep and sincere appreciation of the miracle of running water, you need to have walked down the path to the little house in a cold rain. Water was good even when it had to be lugged in buckets, but it seemed more miraculous when it appeared in lavish quantities with so little effort.

Isaiah tells us that God's gifts, pictured as water, are more lavish than even the bounteous flow from modern plumbing. Isaiah 41:17 describes out need: we are "parched with thirst." It is difficult for adults to remember that, but it's not for our children. In the back seat of a car, thirst sets in just past the 5-mile mark of a 10-mile drive. We grownups are seldom aware of being thirsty.

Yet our tongues are parched. We will die without the water God provides. And God does provide. Creator God makes rivers from nothing. Great plunging rivers, radiant with rainbows of color and spumes of white water. Water enough. But God sends more. Wells in the valleys for those who cannot approach the roaring river. And for those without a bucket or a path to the well, there will be pools in the desert.

In the pools, children play. Tired people bathe dusty, calloused feet. The sick are brought for healing and rest. Wherever a blessed sickroom is tucked into a caring corner, wherever children color and paste and learn, wherever friends gather in quiet sanctuary around the Word, there are the pools of water.

With such a gift of life-giving water, can there be more? Yes! Greenness and growth around the pools of water: cedar acacia, myrtle, olive, cypress, and pine trees. Green fragrant growth, shade and life, protection, and beauty. "How? When?" we ask.

Streams from arid heights, wells and pools have a life-giving, life-sustaining, love-from-God explanation. "The holy Lord God of Israel created it all" (Isaiah 41:20 Contemporary English Version).

Remember the water pails and count your blessing! Remember your baptism and give thanks!

# Acknowledgments

Marj Leegard wrote all of the columns in this book for her "Give Us This Day" column in *Lutheran Woman Today*. The column titles and original month of publication appear below, following the same order as the table of contents.